This Book Belongs To

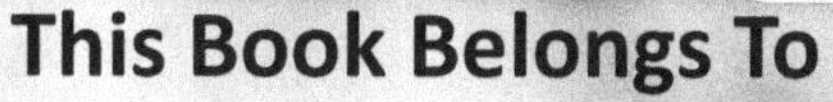

____

This Book Belongs To

Easy Planners And Journals
To help you organize your life

This book is copyright protected.
Reproducing this book is prohibited
and not allowed without the
permission of the author. All rights
reserved.